Kink and Particle

for Barrie and Michèle

Kink and Particle

Tiffany Atkinson

seren

Seren is the book imprint of
Poetry Wales Press Ltd
57 Nolton Street, Bridgend, Wales, CF31 3AE
www.seren-books.com

First published 2006
Reprinted February 2009

ISBN 978-1-85411-434-1

A CIP record for this title is available from the British Library.

The publisher acknowledges the financial assistance
of the Welsh Books Council.

Cover: Fossil (c) 2006 by Sally Weber
A pulsed light image using holographic interferometry
to reveal the hidden motion of breath, blood and muscle tension.
www.sallyweber.com

Printed by RPM Print and Design

Contents

TEA

You made me tea
while I shook the rain from my jacket.
You stooped to fit into the kitchen,
but handled the cups as if they'd been
the fontanelles of two young sons
whose picture sits in the hip of your 501s.
We spoke of – what? Not much.
You weren't to know how your touch
with the teaspoon stirred me,
how the tendons of your wide, divining hands
put me in mind of flight.

You wouldn't have known
when you bent to tend a plant
that your shirt fell open a smile's breadth.
You parted the leaves and plucked
a tiny green bud. Best to do that
with the early ones, you said.
I thought of the salt in the crook
of your arm where a fine vein kicks.
Of what it might be like to know
the knot and grain and beat of you;
the squeak of your heart's pips.

ADULT THINKING

Take, for example, this beach: more a stretch of pigskin
swabbed with flies, and scarcely the place to savour your ice-cream
or chips, much less knuckle down with a lover, less still
to bring your kids; the sea itself a disc of hammered tin
with a corpsy tang and rusting, lethal edge; but the truth
is it's late, there's an ache in the pan of your back,
and with no-one to tell you better, you barely care
that the flies don't know you from carrion, not when this rock here
has just the curve to fit your spine so your upturned face
gets a widescreen gape of sky, and if the sun were to come round,
well, you'd be there for the taking; so it strikes you
as you spark up one of the cigarettes you quit last week
that you're settling for less these days, that, at the same time,
there are worse, no, infinitely worse things.

ACTS OF DEVOTION

Frances cleans teachers' cars
for Christian Aid week. She carries the bucket
in numb white knuckles to the red MG
that Robert drives – Rob, the lab-technician,
chosen by the nuns, no doubt, for buck-teeth
and shyness: Rob, for whom Frances is a candle
burning both ends. Her knees buckle down
in the grit, and she scrubs the bits that no-one
ever dreamt to scrub till the water runs ferrous.

Behind the hedge in the Rosary Gardens
a sister whistles. Frances thinks of an evening
after mass when, itchy for sin, she slipped
through the gate to the sisters' quarters. And there,
the crazed old nun who spat dirt and argued with bushes,
who, rumour had it, was tethered by a length of rope
to the kitchen taps, was perched like a broken kite
on the compost heap, caught for that instant
in the bullseye of the looming hillside crucifix.
When she raised her blessing hand to Frances' head
she was spreading her knees to piss, a hard gold curve
like Frances' father made by the bothy last summer:
the smell of hot copper, raked leaves.

Frances wrings out the sponge, her stinging
fingers laced with suds. Now she sees the cut
in her palm from the rust: the two, three, four now,
drops, like pomegranate seeds, caught
on her cuff and held for the weft to cherish.

PHOTO FROM BELFAST

I knew him, the dead boy, Michael.
Only for three hours, maybe, taken in all.
He stopped me for a light outside my local –
I fell for the accent, the smile. I'd no particular errand
that August Saturday, and stood him a pint.
It was one of those conversations you have perhaps
twice in your life; in full-flash, polaroid.
I was the one took his picture on the Queen's Road,
after he took mine. We were both half-cut by then.
The car was a chunk of dark, behind and to his right.
Blue, maybe black, dead shiny. I'd a new pair of jeans on
and clocked my shape in its panels on the way in.

I'd have stayed for the fourth pint, only
I was mulling over a pair of spike-heels I'd taken
a shine to a while back. Truth is,
when the car put a root of white heat through the tarmac,
made light of the pub, and punched out the street
in a riptide of splinters, I was three blocks east
with his number tucked in my backside pocket
and my heart set on a pair of fuck-me shoes;

and that has a way of shifting your focus,
making you rethink your image. Since I heard
they'd turned up his camera, since I saw the footage,
I've been framing everything in split-seconds;
shutter-speeds, degrees of exposure. I develop him
nightly from the reeling dark – each particular fluke
of space, time, matter. You'd not think it difficult,
to filter him down through the pinhole of morning,
to bring him back to light, to get the picture.

PADDLING

My grandmother stands on the sea's lip,
a weathered Aphrodite
in an oyster-coloured mac.
Beyond her the egoless blue
flickers with sails.

My father and I hang back.
We expected Sunday clothes,
a sheer drop to a grievous sea,
a scattering as of confetti. Instead
she shucks her shoes and popsocks
and I glimpse her feet for the first time:
pale Victoriana on the packed sand.

It's early March. The water
bites her ankles as she wades
through bladderwrack and flotsam,
lifting her hem above the breathing swell.
She casts his dust on the webbed foam,
watches the teak box fill and sink.
Gulls work the sky like scissors.
A day made for sailing, and his dinghy
gone for a song to a London couple
with three kids and a hatchback.

She turns, and the low sun
strikes her eyes' flint.
There are traces of what might be ash
on her damp shins, but we say nothing.

FOR A HOUSEWARMING

For our garden keeps its flint heart
in weeds. For we've crawled all morning
with iron and blade, and barrow and spade
can hang for a workday. For these are holidays.
For the neighbours play tangos in the back yard
and booze through the long arc of the afternoon.
For you drive out for wine and tobacco
and I breathe the kitchen's vapour:
hot potatoes, bruised mint, lamb roasting
slowly away from its bone. For up in the high room
there's a bed made ready like a revellers' table. For there
we'll undo ourselves against raw board and plaster.
For we all feel the heat. For thunder sounds the valley now,
jamming the radio's quiet groove. For pigeons on the eaves
take fright now; beating softly down, down.

STROKE

So I drive for the first time this season,
grinding gears like a bonesetter
through two counties, keeping
a headful of place-names, popsongs,
advertising jingles, anything.

You're half-in, half-out
and spare as a zen parable.
Your tongue lifts like gold-leaf
when I lean in to decipher.
Old seducer, your eyes knit light

to the same, cruel, Saxon blue. I
know you, walking without help
like a dowser, astonished by your own
feet. You've no mind for the practical,
but it won't wait. I'll be clearing

the cottage as-soon-as, wearing
the plaid shirt you kept for the roses,
dosing myself with the brandy, which
you'll not miss. I'll be every bit as ruthless.
Your neighbours are sheer concern,

warning that the half-read book,
the teacup, the biscuit missing a bite
are hardly a job for a woman in my state.
Their sprung smiles bay for a lick
of the old hurt, but I won't have it.

ZUPPA DI CECI

In chipped English she told me
that to get mine like hers   Well
    I'm just too flash-in-the-pan
These things take time   Chick-peas alone
    must be soaked overnight   then simmered for hours
while you stand at the stove with a slow spoon
    skimming off scum   only then a hope in hell
you'll get the rest of the ingredients to sit
    on the right staves   Though
what this has to do with you
    slipping out in the crease of night like
a dropped stitch   I can't think   just
    the kitchen window's black slab
where I stand sucking cream from the lip
    of an old spoon   a platter of reheated stars
and last night's moon served cold

TAXI DRIVER, SEPTEMBER 2001

Outside the cinema
you put on American rage

and hardly expect it to fit you like buckskin
or give you a whiff of distant slaughter,

only now I'm walking home with Travis Bickle
high on the kick of weaponry

cocked in his body's oiled sockets,
staring his own reflection out in shopfront glass

while I flutter like Betsy in my chilly
origami frock. But it's little, ribby Iris,

wide-eyed, stoned as the woman taken,
sizing you up from under her floppy-brimmed

hat, that gets you most. Now you take aim
from the foot of the bed, rehearsing the things

a 44 magnum can do to a woman's face,
and worse. You're joking, of course,

but then, that's muzzle at my throat,
and baby, you I'm looking at.

SUDDEN PAST

Sleep's reckless. Daytime
we're strangers, but that shirt
now I'd know anywhere, each last
crease and plane. What broke
from the smelt of dream. *Rubella*,
you whispered. And *ex patris*. Which
struck home like the hot jagged reek
of creosote on an August afternoon,
as true to the grain. And two years
behaving like strangers, how funny,
with hindsight... well, I was, in fact,
about to point this out, when *Bird*, you
said, which proved our sudden past, for
they called me that as a child, *two things,*
Bird: not everything out there loves us,
and we're neither of us in our right mind.

PORTRAIT PHOTOGRAPHY

There: on the left wall of the studio
where the sun strikes full and loud –
the photographer's firstborn, hoist
like a tuber of light from her element,
her mother laid out as earth for rain
and doctors receding like so much apparatus
from the shock of her, her spanking vowels.
The world expands to take the live charge in.

And slowly, from the other, unlit side
a figure devolves from shadow, only
a cigarette smouldering back to her lips
for accessory. Face to the corner of the room
she makes a closed, unbreakable circuit,
one hand finding itself in the dark fork of loin
as the flesh comes into its own. And here,
in the awkward space between,
I pull myself together for the taking: not
like my family's women, sharp and well-composed,
but accidental, bookish, pushing thirty.
Let that be the truth then; taken, told.

AUTOBIOGRAPHY WITHOUT PRONOUNS

Driving back in the slipstream
of the windfarm, each arc of white-
through-blue reaping ohms from clean
air. The sky would be priceless but
for a hairline crack on its far curve:
everything in slo-mo, the sea
for miles on the passenger side
like the hiss of Super-8. Feathers by
the roadside. Breaking home for twilight
where the traveller selling quartz hearts
on the seafront prophesies a wild affair
and light rain, though in no particular
order. The small girl rounding the corner
on a scarlet tricycle has just created
pigeons; an astonishment of beat and wing.
Mother's death was nothing unexpected
but Ricardo's came brutally. Pan through
sky to sea to road to quartz to pigeons
as the last train westward claxons in. All
change. And love insists, like gravity.

MOTHER IN DREAMS

My mother in dreams, dressed
like a refugee with penny-blacks where
her eyes should be, says in a TV voice
now, girl, what took you? Her forehead
franked with hurt as I lick her eyelids
shut and double her back through the tight
slit of the two-up-two-down-town-house
where my stepmother crackles with static,
cross-legged, purified, and fat with imminent
delivery. Must return my mother's skin,
the slow cyrillic of that unschooled hand.
Wake tangled in that cord, or choke
on words that just won't cut it.

BABYSITTER

So you count out an hour
in five-minute segments of pizza
till her cry beats in semibreves
down two flights.
You carry her out like salvage,
barefoot over sheer floors
to the kitchen's chill. Against
your denimed hip she's all surface
and roll, a live weight, light packed
into her in fistfuls. She brims and kicks
while you fumble with formula, teaspoons, Calpol –
she's the expert here, and knows it.

Down through a decade's empty rooms
your mother's disappointment
falls in crisp pleats.

DAD, DOWSING

Already he's there, the crisp lawn snapping
at his fat boots. While he broke and sheared
the birch twigs I, no doubt, was doing something
trivial – applying lipgloss, say, or whisking *latte*.
And that's just so like the both of us. He smells
of shed – of engine oil, waxed jackets, turpentine.
I think he's why I like men to be men; and why I
don't. The twigs make sudden wingbones. As
my heels sink through the mud I cannot say who
is the least ridiculous. Our mutual adulthood a late
embarrassment. And whether this hocus-pocus works
or no, we'll flicker at each other over mugs of tea
and he'll say, what's the story then – this guy
that rings at all hours, keeps you up at night? And
something like an aquifer may tremble imperceptibly
and I'll say, no big deal, dad. Honestly. It's nothing.

FIRST PETS

Someone starts a game which gives us
each a porn-star's *nom-de-guerre*. It calls
for mothers' maiden names, involves first
pets. Like mumps, most of us had them.
How I begged, and when she came, my puppy's
helplessness appalled me. Poor incontinent
I couldn't love – how like me – craven, brutish,
always to the heel of things –

       – dogs scare me still, like slugs,
like kids; the same uncertain grasp of species.
Dreams deliver me of litters, mewling
snub-nosed pups I cannot feed, and carry
in their cauls from door to door –

and 'Mitzi Farmer' lives her porn-star life
in cul-de-sacs like these, uncertain
for the most part what's fuck, what's fight.
I'd say she falls late to bed with furry creatures
stitched just to be held. Her mother seldom
calls. Mitzi has a proper knack with animals.

FAMILIES BEING ENGINES

theirs ticks over like a cat deep in a basketful
of linen. Boys brood handsomely from room
to room while we work through first white,

then red, then the inevitable Jameson. The poet
in oblique white and his wife who laughs hot
coals. Beyond us Portnoo cedes its light. Talk

overlaps on homes: your Derry pile scrubbed
bare and left that afternoon; my flat three hundred
miles away where ficus leaves skate down the

draughty hall; my father's twenty-seventh house,
etc. Form and content: what a bloody mystery. I'd
no more let my roots grow raw and dark than fly,

my mother said, who flitted army-quarter twenty-
whatever without so much as a by-your-leave. And
yet a person is the space they spare for those they

love. Next morning, weary, and for fearing I may
not love wisely – well, I weep neat whiskey through
four counties, all the long green way to Dublin.

TESTIMONIAL: ISCARIOT

Fathers, elders, only
consider it this way. The act so mortally simple,
a child's task. His cheek as warm bread; a touch of salt
about his mouth, a delicate scratch of herb. My palm
against his clean breast. Caught between the taking-leave
and having done, a fraction ahead of the tiny event
no merciful g-d would allow. Believe, there was faith
on my tongue, through all the hours the lamps were bright,
the doors ajar, while meat and wine passed hand to hand
that final Pesach night. He was morbid, subdued. We
all thought it due to the wine, knowing him to be untouchable:
through him slipped miracles. But, fathers, elders,
let it be said how he knew, even then, it was as good as done;
and of flood, or bolt, or burning bush, came none.

THE ANATOMY LESSON OF
DR NICOLAES TULP, 1632

Hanged for thieving a coat in the raw new year
Adriaenszoon lies on the slab for Dr Tulp.
The doctor takes the stage in sweeping gallows black
as the good guildsmen of Amsterdam flock round
in a quackery. This Tulp has a feeling for light
and shade. Behold how he unpicks the knot
of the offender's left hand, the insinuating scalpel
paring back skin like the peplum of a tulip. Such
immaculate work: the smooth-cheeked spectators
press in, anaesthetised by high, white ruffs, purveyors
of tendon and carpal. With watchmaker's nicety,
Tulp applies forceps to the *flexorum digitorum*,
and the dead man's hand becomes fist. All is decorum
as the deadpan Doctor makes a case of Adriaenszoon.
The gentlemen, for the most part, keep their corruption
at arm's length. Tulp's in up to the neck. Between them
they'll have two coats off the poor man's back.

QUANTUM THEORY FOR BEGINNERS

Energy can be transferred from one form to another
    so tell me you didn't feel that
but the total energy of a system is constant
    yes even from here
this is absolutely true in classical mechanics
    true I felt that absolutely
yet in quantum systems the value of energy fluctuates
    naturally
and fluctuation has real physical consequences
    our flesh is more than the sum of its working parts
the barrier penetration during alpha decay of nuclei is one case
    the one beneath my bed with spare shirts in it is another
we will meet alpha decay in Chapter 8
    my love we are none of us invincible
we have already encountered barrier penetration in Chapter 1
    one might yes put it something oh yes relatively like yes that

BIRTHDAY

A woman of thirty needs
to surprise herself. Her cat
does what comes naturally
in effortless syllabics.
A woman of thirty smokes
all morning, sips espresso
so strong she can taste her heart-
beat through it. The bad taste of
hearts. That fist of gristle which
has yet to punch its own weight.
That soufflé stashed in the high
heat of the chest, obliging
good humour for its proving
or its pratfalls. Thirty-year
olds sense they're nothing special.
All loneliness is like theirs.

UMAMI

Take strawberries: a hearty basinful
you should have picked yourself. Wipe and hull
and quarter, one by one. Drop in a *bain-marie*
with an inkling of sugar, and leave them
to express themselves. They will hang
in muslin overnight, giving up a slow pulse.

Now bring wine to the boil's brink.
Flame it to draw the acid's splinter. And
distil the whole lot down with citrus pulp
to a mellow pool. Be prodigal with pepper
and quicken with vinegar. The briefest glint
of chilli, shot of orange flower water. You

are aiming past salt, sweet, sour, bitter, for
umami, the elusive fifth sense. Mouth-feel,
shimmy of molecules over the tongue's bulbs,
riff through the nasal caves. Hit of crimson
glimpsed at the corner of the palate's eye,
a late wave breaking low in the throat.

Plain bowls are best. The squeak of white
against that ribald red. Anoint each meniscus
with a glam of olive oil. Cast rose petals over.
This is not to be served up lightly. Come
to the table with a clean slate, warm from a day
lived well-enough through, heart in full spate.

QUEEN OF THE LEAD GUITAR

I'm making you a tape
    he says. You'll hate it
(now he's got her full
    attention), since you're
not the sort of girl who
    gets the lead guitar. This
after two Rioja evenings.
    But it's true that Tallis,
thinking less in bars
    than aeons, who laid
planes of sound so close
    you couldn't slide a key
between them, 's what she
    had on in the car. She asks
if he can play guitar like it's
    his childhood sweetheart
wedded to his best friend.
    He's his real age then:
the jacket sloughed up past
    his ears, the shredding grin
and fingers pliéed round
    a roll-up, boy-oh-boy. She
leans in, fires his cigarette,
    removes a hair of hers
that frets there.

WORST CASE SCENARIO:

It's not just me, there really *is*
an elephantine envelope folding itself
round the corner. People stop dead
and fumble for their mobiles. Dogs
go mental. It's the smell. That yeasty,
mouldered bloom. Beyond the rotting
church it gathers speed, its scuffed edge
nudging a tinkling moraine of bottles
and flotsam. It's a question of proportion,
but beige on this scale is menacing,
believe me. That, and knowing the address
dragged face-down through the dirt is
mine. My prodigal havoc, gummed edge
rucked to a snarl, rears like a breaker now,
bent on deliverance. And what to do,
but unseal the front door with bare
face, bare feet, breathe, breathe—
and crash through the crackling cellophane
window of thirty years' comeuppance?

SONNET TO HAND-ROLLED
GOLDEN VIRGINIA

You are right. It does come first. White
touchpaper thin as a host, then gunpowder,
fuse, and the rest will follow, sure as breath.
Little Promethean acts that set the world
alight. Ritual origami for the spiritually lost.
Forgive the quick intimacy at bars and parties,
for we know each other in the lung, the heart;
smoke-screen wizards all. And I a good enough
person otherwise. I take the stairs. Buy vegetables.
Am a paid-up member of Amnesty International.
I hold down a job, between fag-breaks. Angel I am
not. Everyone needs forgiving. So forgive me, but
I won't quit. And if this helps you to overlook my
other, many, far more grave shortcomings, so be it.

COFFEE SHOP, TUESDAY AM

These are the casual lines of mid-workday-morning
sunlight: teaspoons on china, kitten-heeled feet,
and the bright plastic horror of the teething-ring –
my mother's laugh, almost, on the up-beat.
Infants sprout from laps like they might spill,
worn like the sharpest fashions of the season:
their mothers thought I'd be behind the till,
or not sat here, at least, without good reason.
I've come to browse the papers, have a smoke,
but there's buggies double-parked inside the door,
so I'm reapplying lipstick for the bloke
I picked up in a bar the night before. He's
tall, unshaven, half-dressed for the fun of it,
reeking of sex, as it happens, and they're having none of it.

ONLY SO MANY WAYS

to slip Cambridge into conversation,
surely; when its junkies and pram-faced teens
cling by hangnails to each soft embedded
clause. And me, I've had nothing since
breakfast: I need to order, not deal snippets
of Stevens over appetizers. Honestly. Your
guts work just like any other. Ach, macrobiotic.
I work my cigarette like pornography. Thus each
of us stakes out our clichés. And yet you're not

my enemies. You know the horrors of the small
hours, and your bodies too will fail you. How
do we imagine otherwise, talking Chablis over
Chardonnay, and trying with each overstated
preference to give mediocrity the slip? As if.
We pay, secrete an unflamboyant tip. I see
there's a glass or two left in the bottle, and
someone remarks to the effect that if anyone's
going to smuggle sour grapes out, it's me.

YNYSLAS

And the high, eaves-
dropping wind
all night on the roof's
black keys. Waking
rocked by tide; the soft
flesh-bells of cattle, gull-cry
winching up the boatyard's
dirty beats, synaptic crack
of cock-crow. And the sky's
live tissue duplicates itself.
He's shattering goose eggs
into a havoc of sun as she
packs her soft red bag and
scales the gears, her head too
full of light, or heat, or dust.

ABERYSTWYTH SHORT FICTION

And if there's a punchline, it's
police tape cordoning the lamp-post
by the deli, the police patrol all day

as folk baffled past with parcels of
pastrami, all because someone's Jack
Russell cocked its wee leg at a kink

of faulty circuitry. Wham-bam! Kentucky
fried. Unlucky. But a moral for the loose-
flied lads in the Llew Du there, who'll

never know how close they came. And if
there's a subtext, it's Friday next, the small
hours outside Spar, my mate and I barely

in possession of our own names, the whole
street boxed off by the dark italics of police
and students hanging from their third-floor

windows, some kinda bust-up, same old
same old, move along now please, and what
you'd miss with all the flash and grab. Was

someone's girlfriend biting down on some-
one's name. Her face a broken glass where
maybe just that afternoon a brimming cup

had been. And further back or deeper down
beneath. The same moon standing by like
an anaesthetist. The old sea sucking its teeth.

THEN EVERYTHING WAS AXE

Too late in the day, with
(what were we thinking of)

no tent, thunder scuffing
the tips of the hills, we found

that somewhere between the deep
drop down and setting up camp

in an ingrown fold of the cwm,
we'd left behind, mislaid, let

fall or otherwise failed to keep tabs
on the axe. Then everything was

axe: the eighth, ninth, tenth
unstitching of our steps, the pooling heat

and pegged-out sky, each sheaf of grass
each bush turned inside-out... Forget

the quietly perspiring Sémillon,
the raunchy steaks we brought

to toast ourselves, the single heron
pitched like once-in-a-lifetime

at horizon, and the freestyle (what
were we thinking of) sex. Just axe's

invisible plumb-line drawing it all
down like awning, grinding

on the conscience like last words,
distilled to purest form, the shape

of human-frailty-overcome.
Without it, out there, we had

all the personal resourcefulness
of berries. Would you believe I

was searching my own back pocket
when your cry struck out? The palpable

click of a clean fit, of hickory heft
and honed wedge to the shape

hewn inwardly of old-style need,
then world springing back on its axis.

a lover's.
        There, he insists,
a small girl weeps in the corner, and
he'll run himself into the wall for her,
over and over. How can he know his
own strength? Your attempts
to get him back to bed take on the stylings
of Greek drama. In the dream-room
what good – (but you don rationale
like a back-to-front jumper and match
his rhythm; walk him back and
back again and deadlock the door
on the off-chance) –

                        what good
                                daylight
if this time the root
back to the underworld pulls deeper,
pulls him under – and if henceforth
you must visit him down corridors
just long enough for second thoughts,
appearing to him always down
the wrong end of a telescope? Come back,
he says, it's not your turn – (has someone
switched the reels again, or is this your dream?)
Which awakenings to count on, when to act
in good faith, when to let things play
themselves straight, when to ride the long –
and maybe – infinite – illusion out –

NINE MILES STATIONARY:

we stretch from our vehicles like molluscs,
raw flesh bared to a flaring sky. Fair play,
I never figured Swindon for the promised
land. A girl grits her heels on the hard shoulder,
sporting an inexplicable ballgown at high noon.
She spits into her mobile's cut-throat blade,
I fucking said I fucking don't know. And
my father, loving nothing like emergency,
is on the phone too – should've checked first,
should've... Though my life has not, once, yet,

proved urgent. Some kid on the inside lane
can't wait: his mother strips him businesslike
and points his little penis at the verge, even from here
his face a clap of rage. Meanwhile the queue grows
rearwards like a German sentence back to Bristol,
where I stopped to squeeze into my dark dress. Lizzie,
take it as the crow flies, I may have to bury you
out here, though being on time would still have been
too late. Lilies, exhausted, on the passenger seat;
their scent given up on a wreath of my own heat.

BLACK LION PROPHET

He's drunk of course   though not in the modern
way   His style's more oldee testament   Old
nicotine-fingered Moses   picking splinters
of psalm from his teeth   Which isn't to say
he's a nice bloke   or an easy or polite bloke
only   fuck *la politesse*   he's   well he's
good   a grand old cunt   like Gandhi say
or   Winston Churchill even   And the thing
is   is he'll turn what you say on a sixpence
till you don't know head from tail   then slide
his own thoughts in on the backdraft   and
when you're this close to decking him
he does this blessing thing   dead casual   like
he's frisking a fly from your forehead   or
finessing a string quartet through a soft
parabola of Mozart   and he does it   and
you feel your inner contours   sure as whiskey
on a morning-after gut   but deeper   and for one
outrageous moment you could stitch a life
from off-cuts fringed with glory   And that's
how he rakes over your heart's old cockle-bed
or something like it   How he dredges up
and glams such rag-and-bone antiques as
goodness   evil   grace   forgiveness   and
that old fang in the ankle   sod it   love

SINCE

you'd wonder   wouldn't you   why
I allowed the soft tube of myself

to drift down Euston's alleyways
when there were taxis to be had

or kindlier streets   but like I said
or did I   I was quite lost   Red wine

played a part   And then   And how
maybe   he pitched from the wall like

a stolen Picasso   a clamour of dangerous
angles   and all sides bared at once   Did

I slip through a chink of perspective
just in time   or find myself in the station's

acid light   or learn   oh shocking   shocking
that I'd pissed into my own boots   Was it

that night that the tv spilled the secrets of
the mile-deep sea   its fuck-machines and

million little killings   or another night perhaps
all hotel nights the same   No   it was all

American sex as I ran the bath   I remember
now   those high-strung thighs   the men

falling in from all sides   yes   my ruined
boots   and sex   in noirish motels

FOUR POEMS FOR

I

    But no-one—
no-one throws the curveball of your Aberystwyth
    accent—no-one owns
the smoking junkyards of your hands
    —On Keppel St
how chuffed the ornamental cherries are—
    and I all petals—

II

You work on me   but not
like bombs or speeches   More
as sunlight works the coiled springs
of cells   Metaboliser   enzyme   More
than that   just ask me what I wouldn't
do   Ach! Impossible   says the brain's
refusenik   shuffling caveats   stripping
down the moving parts of verbs and
pulling off the old equations   See? Im-
possible
      But not so   say hosannas of petals
          say miscellanies of leaning cells
             Not so

III

What we start with   Fathers—
what we both know about—
How's yer—Who's yer—and
the old lines of begats   All our
childhoods' unkind haircuts
—And your own kids—growing
sharply outwards   less like flowers
than crystals   —First I saw you
with your daughter   At the kerb
she grasped your sleeve   —Her
fierce faith   What is not to love—

IV

And all your secrets   So I'm
made of glass then   if it was my
job   well   wouldn't I sort your
hands' fluttering dossiers   Here's
what I heard   You are just
like the rest of us   give or take
And if there is a bottom line it's
this   We feed each other with
this awkward spoon   or starve

NIA, JUNE 16

But could've been sisters! Mothers
gone the same way, funny that –
and don't we see the funny side,
ova and ova. And that's the down
and dirty of it. Happy birthday, darling.
Time to slough the long soft hurt
of girlhood, wake up to the fuck-it-all-
grandeur you were born to. And,
for the record, anything: a kidney,
half my blood, my husband, if I
had one. That, and a few other
things we can count on, girl. Like
taxes. Death. A Chardonnay hang-
over. Heels. A damn good haircut.

IN THIS ONE

he comes from the garden wearing
nothing but an armful of swiss chard.
His hair curls to the collarbone, and he
has earrings in, for something with each
movement quips back light. And not
a slight man, no. A planetary type. His
skin has sun in its unconscious, not like
mine. He's whistling, bright and abstract.
I am certain he is not from hereabouts.

Of course, I have no garden. Still,
a vase of lilies streaks the air with scent
like spilt milk. And he's all for conversation.
Though my tongue's a husband in a dress-
shop, he does not mind. I could like him,
as it goes. And he could mix a margarita
blindfold. Once he asks, what were you up
to, when I found you here that morning?
I was only writing. Look. A likely story.

RE: VENUS

Setting Year Nine to write about a place
they love, I think of your brother's dripping
doorstep, which I don't love, him neither,
but he sets your Tadcu's telescope in the road
despite the ferret, the baby, the eighth smoked
already; and it's Venus, specifically, I don't
see, which has little to say about meaning while
Morrissey busks through the outdoor speakers,
the boys roll butterfingered spliffs and hawk
love, albeit in not so many words, and I'm all
for your white shirt spooking the damndark road,
a vixen's cry (which might yet be the squeak
of a back door, somebody calling the cat home),
the spark of your lighter; the closer constellations.

NO WARNING:

we are fiercely drunk, and cruelties crackle
like old roses. Bed of thorns. How little
it takes to overturn the pliant geometries
of sex, to lose the nerve of loving. Not

the love itself. The nerve of it. The salmon's
flex against the river-muscle, the insane
faith of the bud. All things that push against
the private and particular. It's the tread
of borrowed boots, your leaving; but I do

not love you less for that. The moon takes
the objective view, posts bulletins across
the bed. And dawn is all mouth. Come back,
and we'll plant the old resentments out. Brew
dodgy wines come autumn. Laugh. Grow fat.

WOMAN RUNNING

All runs rehearsals. For that
final loosening of breath, un-
bolting of flesh from what's
known. Tap open any runner's
knee-joints, learn the rise and fall
of her home town, how she braces
herself for desire: its reach, the bite
of its climbs. For this she lives the
also-rans of most days. Don't expect
thanks. She is running to escape you
all. Her blood's flag beats high, and
her heart's (for now at least) her own.

PERSISTENT COUGH

This cough... they can't
account for it. No symptoms
but the weird aeolian chord
that rips open sleep like a brown
paper envelope. No pain and it
expresses nothing, but I'm full
of the great outdoors. Blame that
indigo Sunday, a bright day cut
on the bias and spliced with wind.
I ran for miles, had spent a night
with you, was jangling with love,
had not resumed my safe Euclidian
shape. I breathed wind and it stayed
in. Elsewhere, surely, a displaced
umbilicus of air describes my inner
space just so: a local sensation on
the scale, say, of a whorl of petals
or a moment's funnelled breeze. Still
all night through I sound my pulmonary
bells, and the outside moves in me.

FELL

Less a daily run   this   than a reckoning
Where Dartmoor empties westward

push out   Strike your heels against
the world's slow turns   Let the love-

me-love-me-not of each stride pull you
clear of ramblers and their idiotic dogs

and be the last thing moving for the blunt
sheep   shear of lark's wing   world made

over   You   weighed down with neither
coin nor key   pay dues in body-salts

the slow exhaust of climbing each turn's
curve into its inverse   unto sky   Now all

skies in particular will take coordinates
from this one   By the heartstrings' drawing

tight you recognise the drag of earth on
air   the old pull underground   the deep wish

spelt in tumuli   And yet the wind's broad
lung!   you cannot help but spread your finger-

tips to thrill it   Never mind how far   how far
back   Should you never turn up there again

you wouldn't think it terrible   to burn down
in the lap of the mineral love   of some god

ANTHURIUM

Bring me the tender
obscenity of petal-tongues

and stamens. Fuck me as light,
by way of kink and particle:

by this we learn our animal.
Fancy the deep seed

singing in the cunt which is
the curved earth's cunt. Like stars.

And do it as you dreamt it through the want
of boyhood, anything,

your birth-right, mine,
the yen of cells. Against

the fall, the hinge of sleep,
the boulder of work to be rolled

from the door each morning.
O, the open-mouthed affirmative.

DALEKS

Back from the time-wars
like sixties kitchenettes *en pointes*,
and suicide bombers all. Scaling
Darwin's stairs a flight at a time
on human DNA, as if that should
be extraordinary these days. And

the Doctor's signed out of the series,
so it's showtime. Wartime. Bigtime.
The sets expand like space itself
to take the implications in. What
intergalactic temperospatial pyro-
technic brouhaha could take us

by surprise, unless our own pasts
twist beneath those clunky lids, with
one eye stalking out the future where,
and let's be frank, things turn out pretty
bleak? Come on. It's not for kids.

THE MAN WHOSE LEFT HAND THOUGHT IT WAS A CHICKEN

did some things remarkably well, like
catching flies and finding dropped earrings
or contact lenses. Others – making omelettes
say – he learned to perform with his left hand
deep in a pocketful of seed. Mere incidentals
if your arm does chicken from the elbow down.
At times, for sure, sheer cock: up well before
he was, especially if his woman was in town,
cock-hand was known to arc at strangers in the pub
or jump soft objects. Shopping for fruit with cock-
hand was no joke. But there was hen-hand too,
heat-seeking, full of mild compulsions. This bird
knew a thing or two about the secret berries of
his lover's flesh, the dust-bowl of her back. And
rumbled the acorn growing in her breast, and fluttered
at her cheekbones till she slept. Then for the kids
alone, the crazy bantam-hand of knock-knocks,
now-you-see-its. Still. To say the sun's play through
his fingers made the brightest comb, to say he
crossed the road more often than required, to say
he only ever drove an automatic, never got promoted
and was photographed more often than he liked, to
say he almost had his own eye out a hundred times
is not to say the man was not his own man. No. He
was a flock of tangents and surprises. And without
him we have lost all memory, all possibility of flight.

COCKEREL-MAN AND THE ROYAL
DONKEY DUCK

's what sir was, yomping up from the street
three sheets downstream and real medieval
arsefaced on his hobby-frog, ohlordy aint
nobody like him for a blue steam. Duchess!
he piped through the moon's horn, hair like yours
grows twice in a lifetime and your lipbones how
they seize me. Then he fuzzed from the head down,
swinging on my neighbour's perpendicular. Open
your smile my mouse, cried he, quite the rivergreen
elvis at that angle, be my spiff and I'll raddle
your bud for good. Yes truly. Thus his pageant
hooked its barrel to the wind. And oh my offal
gan glow tender (albeit known better on the back-
look) for the bold highriding and the heartwhip
and, it must be said, his droll feet. It was close,
as garlic. But. I wheened, you strike the same tune
off the flint of cold day and I'll kindle. End of.
Though it seems to be he's sheer carouse and no thumb.
Where he pearled is only what the wind shook up four
days since. Dropsy crops, they say, blow all stalk.

ALWAYS ONE,

with sprigged comb pricking like a bookmark
from the moment's centrefold. A gimlet
eye that all events must pass through. How

that sweetly shit-and-straw stink stitches up
the elemental. The saurian claw beneath the spat,
the down and dirt of wishbone. To the geometry

of pecks: each flightless tilt at earth describes
our own hypotenuse. The lowly zen of body-mass
v. hours-to-eat-per-day. The clamorous beak of sex.

And iterability of chickens. O little gazebos!
One day's chicken always fresh-hatched from the last
heart's chicken, battening down in the ovoid dust.

SUDDENLY

you're on a train east
with a failing phone, in pain,
another country,
and no more yourself than the moon.

A death. A death.
How nothing in the world will take you in.
At work I am pointless. Ahead is the dumb plain
of grief, the management of grief. It is like

drought. And love, it takes a knocking.
What instincts would not retreat?
That one of us must be the last's
the clutch, the cleave,

and something of this ache between.
The birds at dawn are one-hit bloody wonders.
Find something else to clean. Iron clothes.
Bite down on silence. Make the heart's world turn.

COULD I

Good lord now why not, so come then, crazy degas-
headed man, from your jazz-hands Barcelona, Miquel.

God knows what we'll do with you. The soft instep of Wales has
one deli to speak of and there's precious little architecture, Miquel;

though my friends are irresistible in any dialect. Hell yes,
outside the Nag's Head, finesse that rich cigar, Miquel

and say you're not after the one face you can't place at home!
Your body fibrous as a knuckle of root ginger: how you laugh, Miquel,

like bushfire. Yes then, giant man of childhood cut loose –
I will show you all the things I hold close here, Miquel.

It will be marvellous to see you. I've not told them, yet.
I cannot tell how fine your grasp of ambiguity in English is, Miquel:

T, how happy to be listening from you. I would not mind to be in Whales.
I make the pictures as a present for the one who listens. Kisses. Miquel.

ENEMY –

how gentle we were,

that I know the worm in your gut
like my own. The meat of my hate

grows toothsome these days. I am
never bored. Each breakfast a triumph
and my dear friends more than rubies.

Never come even. I'll turn your children
into clutch-bags. Eat you blue. Your mother
will wish herself a doorstop; your ancestors
root themselves up at the bone and hurl fireward.

Truly, I will see to you like smallpox
dressed as a bailiff whose daughter you jilted
for his wife, the morning he got fired for smoking crack
to forget the tumour. All your exes will be watching. Lights
blown out... taps running blood... Anything might happen.

HEY LOVE –

She hawks in your wineglass. On your
banker's handshake and your cheap suit. Says
you use language like a wanker's handkerchief,
that all you gave her was the depths of her insides;

and since you're asking, yes, she'd rather be dead
unmissed for five days with her face gnawed off
by cats than one of your lot. Lordy me, she never
used to be extreme. We had her down as a sound one,

good in a crisis. Like potatoes. So she's keeping
schtum about you-know-what, that's her mother's side,
but don't light that cigar just yet. Remember Philippa?
Oh she remembers you, and she's not nearly as much

fun as I am. Call her sometime, boy she'd love to chew
the fat. Here, use my lighter. Childhood, blah-de-blah,
we know. Don't shoot the messenger. And don't go taking
me for anyone who gives a shit. See? Through, *so* through.

NIETZSCHEANISM AND THE
MEANING OF THE SUPERMAN

Lights are going on
Out there a million kitchens' busy
knives   the endless declensions of
households   The oedipal types
the satellite types   the serial
lawns of the suburbs   Down
in the street she wants to know whose
jacket's on the back seat   And somewhere
in a pub perhaps   or Seico's tin-can
caravan   your man is raking back his hair
and leaning in to catch what someone's really
saying

          Jesus is that
only birdsong   flung out
like a pocketful of kryptonite
The rooftops quiver through it   Open

windows   It is all your business
This connection   This

Acknowledgements

Acknowledgements are due to the editors of the following publications in which some of these poems first appeared: *The Bridport Prize Anthology 2002* (Sansom & Company, 2002), *The Daily Telegraph, MsLexia, The National Poetry Anthology 2004* (United Press, 2004), *New Welsh Review, New Writing 9* (Vintage, 2000), *Orbis, Oxford Poetry, Poetry Review, Poetry Wales, Pterodactyl's Wing: Welsh World Poetry* (Parthian, 2003), *Seren Selections* (Seren, 2006) and *Skald*, 'Tea' was winner of the Ottakar's and Faber National Poetry Competition, 2000, and 'Photo from Belfast' was winner of Academi's Cardiff International Poetry Competition, 2001.

Huge thanks also to my friends and colleagues in Aberystwyth, Cardiff, Lancaster and Aberdeen, and to everybody at Seren.